A Shadow's Lament

A Shadow's Lament

A COLLECTION OF POEMS

SHEILA RUBY

Sheila Ruby
A Shadow's Lament: A Collection of Poems

Publisher: Sheila Ruby
Text Design: Angela Jiniel LaMunyon
Cover Design: Angela Jiniel LaMunyon
Copy and Line Editing: Kristen Hamilton

A CIP record for this book is available from the Library of Congress Cataloging-in-Publication Data

ISBN-10: 979-8-218-67023-8

Table of Contents:

ACONITUM NAPELLUS

For Julian—

A poet's soul cannot be taught, only discovered.

Your gift for writing, your way of seeing the world,

Has reminded me that stories must be told,

That pain must be spoken,

That shadows must be given their lament.

You inspired this book—

And I know one day, yours will inspire the world.

Introduction

This book is for those who have loved and lost.
 For the ones who carry grief in their hearts,
For those who have made peace with the demons,
    Or those who are still trying to find their way through it.

These words are for the abandoned, the betrayed, the forgotten.
For those who have reached for love, only to watch it slip away.
    For those who whisper into the void, wondering if it ever listens.

This is a journey through grief and ruin,
Through love and the wreckage it leaves behind.
    Through sorrow, survival, and the search for something more.

If you have ever felt broken,
If you have ever longed for something just out of reach,
If you have ever wondered whether healing is possible—
    Then these words are for you.

    May you find something here that speaks to your soul.

Part I:

Before there was loss, there was love.
Before there was silence, there were voices.
But love does not always last,
And voices are destined to fade.

This is where my story begins—
In the absence of those who should have stayed.

Echoes of a Nightmare

I lost my parents to the grasp of time,
Their love, a fading echo, a hollow chime.
Left behind, too young to understand,
Abandoned, a shadow in their unsteady hands.

At three, I learned how love can break,
How promises shatter, how hearts forsake.
They never looked back; no fight, no plea,
Just a quiet goodbye, leaving nothing of me.

I waited for years in a world unknown,
A child adrift, without a home.
Through crowded houses and fleeting care,
I searched for faces that were never there.

No longer will I carry the blame
For their departure, their dying flame.
Yet it haunts me still, when I gaze at my kin—
How could they leave us the way that they did?

I longed for no one but them in my life,
Yet their absence cut deep, a blade, a knife.
The years stretched long; I struggled to mend,
Living with wounds that refused to bend.

There must've been an attachment I once knew,
Maybe fleeting moments when their words felt true.
Naïve and hopeful, a child of dreams,
Before creation unraveled at its fragile seams.

I've sought for answers, though none will suffice—
Their silence remains, a dagger of ice.
Perhaps I should thank them for making me strong,
For teaching me how to survive the wrong.

I built my own warmth from ashes and stone,
For no hand was offered—I stood alone.
But a part of me aches, a part of me yearns,
To
   unlearn
      this
         aching,
           to
              watch it all burn.

Now love finds me, yet I avert its gaze,
For a fragmented heart cannot escape its maze.
How can I give wholly what's shattered in shards,
A soul still imprisoned, behind its own guards?

Yet I dream of a dawn, a glimmer of light,
When this nightmare dissolves into the night.
I'll awaken to find you standing near,
And all the shadows will disappear.

You'll be by my side, and I'll be by yours,
As the torment drifts beyond memory's shores.
This existence of sorrow will fade like a stream,
And I'll know at last—it was only a dream.

The Haunting Flame

Most days, the agony wraps itself around my soul,
A shadowed being, refusing to let go.
Just when I think the inferno is through,

It flares again—a ghost of you.

What you did to me lingers like a curse,
A wound eternal, each recollection rehearsed.
You ruined me, left wounds in my life,
A shattered mirror reflecting my strife.

I look around at all I have gained,
Lucky, they say, to have escaped the chained.
And yet, even in my sanctuary, you remain,
A demon that dances in my brain.

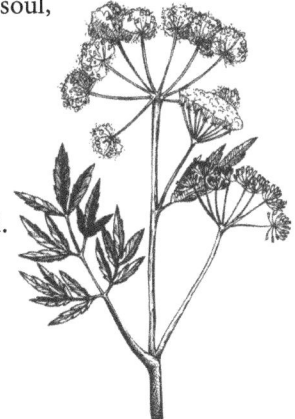

CONIUM MACULATUM

5

Do you think of me, as I think of you?
Does my image haunt, like shadows do?
Part of me hopes, when you close your eyes,
It's my face that stalks your sleepless nights.

But hatred twists its claws within,
For what you did, for what has been.
Yet darker still is the hate I bear,
For myself, for the silence, for the despair.

You stole everything—my innocence, my trust,
Left ashes where dreams once were lush.
I can never forget the shadow you cast,
A torment alive in the past.

I wonder, if fate had twisted a kinder thread,
If we had never met, would my skin have bled?
Would the light of my days burn brighter still,
Or would shadows find me, against my will?

I remember your eyes, so piercing and cold,
Twin abysses, where terror took hold.
Your gaze remains, chiseled in my mind,
A haunting reminder, a curse unkind.

You are the monster that lingers near,
A bloodthirsty presence, feeding my fear.
But one day, this flame shall flicker and die,
And I will rise up, unshackled,
                            beneath

                                    the

                                        darkened

                                                sky.

Losing Sight

I will never be the ideal child
You sought in your dreams, serene and mild.
Perfection is an illusion I cannot be,
For inside, I am ruins—fragility unseen.

I feel your gaze, heavy and cold,
Expecting more than this shattered mold.
I walk the edge where shadows call,
Unwilling to bow, to censor it all.

I won't wear the mask of a docile soul,
Living by rules that swallow me whole.
I'll carve my path, as jagged as stone,
Even if I walk it utterly alone.

I mirror you, each step, each turn,
Your fire, your chaos, your will to burn.
But when I do, it feels so wrong,
The same dance, yet a different song.

Remember, I am but a child still,
Even grown, I will falter at will.
Mistakes will tether me to this fight,
While he—the golden one—will shine so bright.

The other child, your chosen heir,
So perfect, pristine, beyond compare.
He will never wander, never stray,
He'll walk the path in your perfect array.

He will never be wild, never lose sight,
He'll be your salvation, your guiding light.
While I, the forgotten, drift in the dark,
A
    shadow
        cast,
           a
           faded
              spark.

So good luck with the son who will never fail,
While I wear my flaws like a funeral veil.
I'm sorry I was never enough for you,
Never the reflection of what you knew.

I'm sorry I failed, for falling apart,
For the wild edges of my fractured heart.
But no more apologies will I recite—
For losing your love was losing sight.

The Last Plea

I sit alone in the silence of my tomb,
Shrouded by shadows that cling to my room.
Far from the world that etched its scars,
I kneel beneath the watchful stars.

On trembling knees, I whisper your name,
Begging forgiveness, swallowed by shame.
One last chance is all I seek,
To prove myself before I'm weak.

Let the past be buried in the grave it deserves,
A place forgotten, where nothing stirs.
But let the weight of it stay with you,
For only you can bear its truth.

I crave rebirth with each new day,
To cast these sins and stains away.
A soul redeemed, in your light's embrace,
A chance to step from this darkened space.

I know your devotion is a constant flame,
It burns through guilt; it sears through shame.
You do not wield my faults as knives,
But hold them still to spare my life.

For this, I kneel in gratitude and fear,
Your mercy—both distant and near.
I try to mend what I have undone,
But my demons wrestle; they've already won.

How many chances have I betrayed,
Squandered words and promises made?
This time, I will not fail or flee,
I swear it on the life of me.

I am sorry for using your light as my guide,
Only when lost in the dark, to hide.
I beg you now, as the silence screams,
Lift me up from this well of dreams.

Give me the strength to walk once more,
To rise up from the mangled floor.
Accept my plea, show mercy divine,
And grant this wretched soul a sign.

One last chance is all I ask,
To prove my worth, to fulfill my task.
I am not bargaining; I am not contriving,
This is no ruse—I am surviving.

Hear my words as shadows fall,
I offer my heart, my soul, my all.

The Weight of Hurt

It hurts when those meant to love you fade,
Their affection a phantom, vacant and frayed.
It hurts when the ones you trust tear apart
The fragile seams of your battered heart.

It hurts when guilt claws deep at your chest,
A sickness whispering, "You are the jest."
Every shadow seems to scream your name,
The weight of blame, an unending flame.

It hurts to see the ruins behind,
Families fractured, chances confined.
A trail of wreckage I dared not foresee,
Cast away, punished for simply being me.

It hurts to carry this anger alone,
A tempest howling through marrow and bone.
To spend your life with a presence turned cold,
Cuffed to the fury, a grief uncontrolled.

It hurts to crave what will never arrive,
Arms to hold you, to keep you alive.
But the ones you long for, the solace you seek,
Turn their backs, leaving you weak.

The emptiness whispers; the silence grows loud,
A shroud of melancholy as dark as a cloud.
You reach for their hands, but they pull back in fear,
The absence of love, sharp as a spear.

How it hurts to weather this alone,
A shadow unwelcomed, a life overthrown.
Yet even in darkness, I whisper my plea—
A flicker of hope for what might someday be.

Part II:

Some wounds refuse to fade.
Some ghosts refuse to rest.
The past lingers in the quiet,

Waiting for the moment it can swallow you whole.

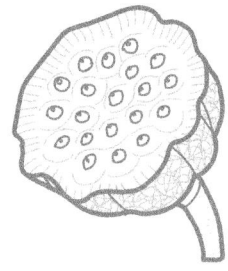

A Shadow's Question

What do you do when whispers of love ring hollow,
When the words wrap you in shackles, yet shadows follow?
They say they adore you, yet their eyes betray,
A hidden truth; another being sways their way.

What do you say when they beckon you astray,
Pulling you down paths where your light fades to gray?
To be torn between two roads, both piercing and cruel,
A puppet dancing, yet never the master of the duel.

How does one act when asked to wear a mask,
When they carve away your life and demand a new task?
They mold you into something that you are not,
Leaving your true self to decay and rot.

You yearn to turn back, to shed this disguise,
To reclaim the reflection in your own weary eyes.
Yet their gazes press harder; their demands constrict,
Your voice silenced; your will afflicted.

What do you do when the verdict is cast,
When they tell you your time has passed?
Their words, sharp as daggers, cut through your core,
And you're left stranded in darkness, alone once more.

The winds howl, and the silence screams,
You clutch at the edges of shattered dreams.
What do you do when the choice is clear,
But the answers dissolve in the shadows near?

You stand in the ruins of what you've become,
A shadow of yourself, your heartstrings undone.
Yet somewhere deep, a flicker remains,
A fire to grapple through the endless pains.

What do you do when all is lost?
You rise up from the ashes, despite the cost.

Darkness

Light dims, the world fades slow,
Stars burn brighter, yet crisp in their glow.
Blackness coils, a slithering stare,
Tightening hands around empty air.

*ATROPA
BELLADONNA*

Haunted Silence

Why do your eyes pierce through me,
And deny the love I crave?
Each time I enter the room,
Your smile begins to fade.

I linger in the shadows of your indifference,
Chilled by a silence that gnaws at my bones.
Am I the sinner in this cathedral of blame,
Or merely the relic of love turned to stone?

I mourn the reflection of the person I was,
A silhouette you no longer see.
The weight of your disdain suffocates,
As if I've been buried beneath the debris.

I want to love you, but how can I?
Your touch is frost; your words, a noose.
Am I the demon in your tragedy—
Or a being you've simply refused?

And yet, this useless pain endures,
A phantom clawing at the edge of my mind.
If you will not hold me, then let the darkness—
Let the darkness

take what you've left behind.

Whispered Hue

I hear your voice in whispered hue,
A shadow soft in morning dew.
Your steps remain though years have passed,
A fleeting breath, a love held fast.
The world is dark, yet I seek you.

The stars still shine, the moon still new,
But none can warm the night's frosty view.
A vision of your passion holds me true—
I hear your voice in whispered hue.

No touch can bring your warmth to light,
No prayer can turn the day to white.
Yet still I walk where once we stood,
Forever lost in all we could.
I hear your voice in whispered hue.

A Letter

I know I'll never see you again,
And your voice will never resound in my life.
Yet I write this letter to the void,
For my body trembles, fragile and rife.

I wish you were here, beside my fears,
To hear the whispers of my dreams and tears.
So few truly know the real me,
And I ache for someone who might truly see—
The shadow of who I long to be.

You'll never know this, but all was for you,
Each step I took, each battle I slew.
I pushed myself to the brink of despair,
Hoping my triumphs might make you care.

I wanted your regret to haunt your days,
For every visit missed, every absent loving gaze.
I thought if I shone like a star ablaze,

I could erase the bitterness of your ways.

I dreamed of the day I'd stand before you,
Bearing the weight of a soul torn in two.
But now I see those dreams were lies,
Empty echoes in storm-filled skies.

Even if I found you, what could I say?
The words would falter, the truth decay.
For you had already carved your scars,
Leaving me alone beneath silent stars.

I hope I am nothing like the shadow you cast,
But if I'm not, will I ever outlast
This feeling that no one truly knows
The aching that within my spirit grows?

I wish I could call you mother,
But the word lies empty, unlike any other.
I longed for you to step from the haze,
To own the wounds you left in my days.

But you remained a phantom, bitter and withdrawn,
And now I'm done singing this same sad song.
I release you to the depths, where shadows dwell,

And bid you farewell in this silent hell.

BRUGMANSIA
ARBOREA

My Past

A lot has been happening lately,
I'm scared out of my mind.
I don't know if I can make it out safely—
My past caught me, pulling me behind.

I try so hard to run away,
But it keeps me trapped inside.
There's so much left I need to say,
But I'm lost in silence, swallowed by pride.

I'm afraid to let it out—
I've held it in too long.
I get so angry, I want to shout,
But the echoes fade before they're gone.

Just when things were going right,
My past came crashing in.
Now I'm crying every night,
Falling back to where I've been.

My heart breaks when I look back,
I pray that when these storms begin,
They won't consume, they won't attack—
That this war won't win again.

I don't know how I've made it through,
This weight that comes so fast.
I wasn't ready for the truth—
For the life I thought had passed.

I'm so lost inside this,
I need a way to fight.
Why can't my life be filled with bliss?
This pain still cuts like a knife.

I'm lost, but I don't want to stay,
I just need a way to break free.
But when I open my eyes and let out my cries,
I am afraid to find—
That my past has trapped and blinded me.

Before Your Throne

As I stand before you beneath your throne,
Will you leave me there to plead alone?
Or will you hear my mournful cry,
A whisper carried on the frigid night sky?

I fought so hard to follow your flame,
Thinking the end was near, yet only the same—
The battle rages, fierce and long,
A tempest where the weak don't belong.

Does strength for an hour become strength for years?
Will you wipe away my joyful tears?
For even joy, in its fleeting grace,
Holds shadows, haunting every sacred space.

Lord, you were bold, a hand outstretched,
Brave enough to save the wretched.
Your bravery, a light in the blackened mist,
Guiding me through the dark abyss.

I know my choices leave scars that burn,
A price I pay for every lesson I've yet to learn.
But I would tread the thorns, accept the pain,
If your hand still pulls me from the rain.

They whisper, "You're not real," a fleeting lore,
Unworthy of devotion, blind to the core.
Yet I've felt your presence, fierce and stark,
A shining light in the endless dark.

You stood me up when shadows pressed,
When depression encased my hollowed chest.
You spoke the words that made me whole,
Breathing sentience into my fractured soul.

Every time I confess my lies,
Your voice interrupts before my cries.
"Forgiven," you say, with omnipotent grace,
As though mercy is inscribed in your timeless face.

The strength to forgive, a strength unknown,
Leaves me in awe before your throne.
How can one so burdened still endure,
To hold the broken, the lost, the impure?

You were brave enough to take this risk,
To pull me from the endless abyss.
Teaching me love in its truest form,
Giving me shelter from life's raging storm.

Now, I am not the same as before,
I've walked through that open door.
Because you dared to take this chance on me,
I stand reborn, no longer bound, but free.

Ricinus communis

Part III:

Love is not a fairytale.
It is fire and passion. It is ruin and death.
It is a curse and a gift.
It gives, it takes, it lingers
in the shadows around you.
And sometimes, it refuses to let go.

When I First Saw You

When I first saw you, my breath was stolen,
A moment stamped in time that could never be broken.
I felt the stars align in the moment I wanted to flee,
As if the universe whispered, "This is meant to be."

Your voice, like a melody, eased my despair,
Each sweet word you spoke opened doors I didn't dare.
When your hand brushed mine, the world grew still,
And my heart, once broken, bent to your will.

I was wounded, a shadow of who I'd been,
Lost in the anguish of sorrow within.
But your arms wrapped around me, steady and strong,
A sanctuary found where I thought none belonged.

When your lips met mine, so soft, so divine,
I felt the spark of our hearts entwined.
Time itself seemed to bow and fade,
As love's gentle fire through the blackness swayed.

You were the light I didn't know I sought,
The shelter I dreamed of but never caught.
You lifted me from the depths of where I'd drowned,
And built a place where no fear could be found.

Your affection was fierce yet tenderly kind,
A flame that burned but never confined.
Where others left wounds, you made me whole,
Giving purpose back to my shattered soul.

I began to live in the warmth of your care,
Free from the burdens I no longer bear.
You promised to shield me, to stand by my side,
And in your tenderness, my fears could not abide.

How perfect and tragic this story may be,
For with you, I learned what it means to be free.

A Cursed Romance

You wove your promises like silken threads,
Binding my ruptured heart as it bled.
I was wounded, lost, drowning in despair,
But you lifted me, whispered adoration into the air.

Your touch was salvation, your words a reprieve,
I looked to the heavens, dared to believe.
Thanking the gods for a second chance,
Unaware I'd fallen into a cursed romance.

But the signs, oh, the signs were there,
A shadow beneath your tender care.
I was blind to the storm that brewed unseen,
An attachment so sweet, yet laced with something obscene.

There was fire in your eyes, burning bright,
A spark that illuminated my world with light.
But day by day, that blaze froze,
Extinguished by lies and secrets untold.

Your words, like poison, seeped into my veins,
A lover's spell that tethered my chains.
My obsession with you made me a slave,
Bound to your darkness, no soul to save.

NERIUM
OLEANDER

Was it love, or was it illusion's snare?
Infatuation dressed in a lover's care?
Perhaps it was both—what does it matter?
In the end, my core was left to shatter.

I was naïve, blinded by trust,
A fragile soul, crumbling to dust.
I would have given you all, my very breath,
But you repaid me with a slow, sweet death.

Why didn't you leave me to fade alone?
Why pull me close, then turn to stone?
The sunlit days dissolved to gray,
The warmth of our intimacy swept away.

You began to stray, a phantom in the night,
Resisting my grasp, slipping from sight.
I fought so hard to pull you back,
But love cannot thrive in the shadow's track.

And so our story ends in tears,
Your promises dead, awakened all my fears.
Now I'm left with a heart in disrepair,
A vacant vessel, empty and bare.

Your spirit lingers, though you are long gone,
Haunting the love that's withdrawn.
You stole the purest parts of me,
And left behind a reminder of agony.

Though I hate the ending, the torment, the despair,
I cannot forget the fire we shared.
A love so twisted, tragic, and cursed,
Forever marked in shadows, my soul immersed.

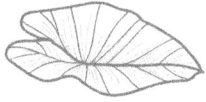

Drowning

Deeper, deeper, I sink,
Water coils tight, filling my lungs.
I try to cry out—only silence answers.
I cannot rescue myself.

My body, heavy. My limbs, frail.
Mouth open, but no sound escapes.
Above, a fractured light flickers,
And suddenly—my body remembers.

Higher, higher, I rise,
Breaking through the surface,
Gasping, trembling—
Breathing once more.

Cruel Embrace

I cannot live without you—
Your absence is a blade, cutting me through.
I try to run, to flee your name,
But each path circles back, always the same.

The love we shared was so true, so divine,
A light in the dark, but a curse intertwined.
Do not ask me to breathe without you,
For my world would turn to ash and my heart would too.

Each day without you is a torment untold,
A slow-burning fire, a grip so bitterly cold.
Years have passed, but the ache remains,
A hurt in my chest, bound in chains.

The heartache builds, taking its toll,
Tearing apart the fragments of my soul.
I cannot stop the stream of tears,
Drowning me nightly, feeding my fears.

Your name lingers in the voids of my mind,
A torment I cannot leave behind.
I wish to be free of your cruel embrace,
Yet I long for the vision of your haunting face.

I love you still—how can this be?
Even as your lies have buried me.
When I learned of another, my heart turned black,
A dagger of betrayal plunged deep in my back.

I thought our devotion was forever dead,
A coffin sealed, a requiem read.
Yet still I crave the poison of you,
The bitter elixir that tears me in two.

Despite all you've done, despite the pain,
I cannot break free from this cursed chain.
Your shadow lingers, a tethered noose,
And I, your captive, cannot cut loose.

My Private Hell

How beautiful, how tragic was our tale,
A love entwined in a beautiful veil.
The passion I craved, the dream I sought,
Yet in its embrace, my heart was caught.

At first, it bloomed, a rose out of fire,
A perfect lie, my savage desire.
The passion burned, the world stood still,
Yet beneath the beauty lurked your will.

Your words, like honey, sweetly dripped,
But in their sweetness, venom slipped.
I was blinded by your fatal glow,
Unaware of the darkness below.

For a time, it seemed eternal, divine,
The love I dreamt of, fierce and mine.
But shadows danced where your gaze fell,
And love became my private hell.

The years pulled us apart like tides,
Yet you returned, the lover that bides.
Your eyes, once warm, now ablaze with flame,
A fire that only knew my name.

Twisted, evil, we played the game,
A dance of pain, a lover's shame.
You pushed, I pulled, a desperate fight,
Caught in the web of shadowed night.

I screamed, I wept, yet I could not flee,
Your hold was chains; I lost the key.
Once I thought I had escaped,
But your shadow returned, my fate reshaped.

A hunter stalking, a predator's grin,
You always found the cracks within.
Toxic love, your gift to me,
A curse disguised as ecstasy.

Yet for all the suffering, the scars I bear,
I wouldn't trade the passion we shared.
For in the torment, the chaos, the fire,
Lies the love I craved, my darkest desire.

Now I vow, under the moon's wicked glow,
No love shall match the one I know.
Your shadow lingers, your fire still burns,

Bound in ruin, a fate I've earned.

Once Upon a Midnight

It's been so long since I could meet your gaze,
The eyes I once knew, now cloaked in a haze.
Sleep eludes me, a whisper in the night,
As I chase the fragments of your fading light.

Once, I was certain I'd perish without you,
A fragile heart bound by a love untrue.
"Forever," you whispered—how sweetly you lied,
But your promises crumbled, and part of me died.

You had a chance to prove your worth,
To anchor me here on this empty earth.
Where were you when the shadows fell?
When I reached for you in this cold, dark hell?

I yearned to hold you, to call you mine,
To feel your warmth in the ice of time.
But your love was a fleeting, dying flame,
A whispered story with no name.

"You're mine," you said, beneath the stars' glow,
Yet you faded away as the tides did flow.
Once upon a time, I believed the tale,
But now you are gone, and I have turned so frail.

You are the phantom I cannot free,
A scar engraved in my memory.
I walk through this wreckage, where our love once grew,
Forever mourning the dream of you.

Taxus baccata

Part IV:

Pain does not mean we are lost.
Loss does not mean love is gone.
We all walk through brimstone and fire,
But even in the aftermath of an eruption, we endure.

Perhaps we are all searching for a way to survive.

Whispers of the Fallen

Angels—beings in shadowed skies,
Known to all, yet shrouded in disguise.
No human hands can grasp their grace,

A touch that fades without a trace.
Their signs remain in fleeting light,
Footprints fading into the night.

Yet their presence is more than a fleeting glow—
They light the flame where darkness grows.

Angels emerge from places unseen,
Disguised in faces both brutal and serene.
A stranger's glance, a fleeting breath,
An absence of life that defies even death.

But beware the ones who leave too soon,
Vanishing under the waning moon.
They come to haunt, to ignite, to scar,
To remind you how fragile we truly are.

Not all angels descend from above,
Not all are bound to mercy or love.
Some will unravel the existence you've sown,
A guide, yes—but to paths unknown.

They're riddles chiseled in time's abyss,
A mystery veiled in shadows' kiss.
Angels, both savior and ghost,
Haunting the hearts that need them the most.

True Love

Love always eluded me—a game of cat and mouse. I would reach for it, feel it brush against my fingertips, only to watch it slip away. I wanted to catch love, hold it still, make it mine. I wanted it to fill the empty spaces inside me, the hollows shaped by years of longing. I thought if I found it, I would be whole again.

Year after year, I spent more time alone, learning to love even the most unlovable parts of myself. It wasn't easy. Love had always felt like something outside me, something I had to chase. But in the quiet moments, in the spaces where no one else could reach, I finally saw the truth.

It was never love that ran from me.

It was my own love I had been missing all along.

HIPPOMANE MANCINELLA

The Demon's Release

I hate you for the ruin you left in me,
The shadows you cast, the chains unseen.
You stole my innocence when I was but four,
And in your grasp, you claimed my soul.

Each day, your name lingers, etched in my mind,
A haunting whisper, vicious and unkind.
The sting you left burns like a flame,
But worse is the trust that you defiled in your name.

I never believed the harm you gave,
Never saw the monster behind the grave.
I handed you power; I gave you my all,
And it took me years to see your thrall.

You were the demon that dwelled within,
A phantom of anguish beneath my skin.
I gave you a home inside my mind,
A sanctum of torment where you confined.

But no longer will I harbor your ghost,
No longer will you feed on what I love most.
Your shadow will fade, your grip will unwind,
For I am reclaiming what is rightfully mine.

Even though the wounds are fresh and sore,
I refuse to let you haunt me anymore.
Your claws have dulled; your power has waned,
And now I rise from the ashes of pain.

I banish you back to the depths below,
No longer in control, no longer my woe.
The chains are broken, your curse undone—
I am free; my battle is won.

Promises Untold

We are fed the illusion of love,
A dream spun from sunlight and rainbows above.
We chase the whispers, the promises untold,
Believing in warmth, in hands to hold.

But love is not gentle; it is wicked and vast,
A creature that howls, a shadow it casts.
Love is a reason to rise each day—
Yet a battlefield where hearts decay.

It is the fight beneath the moon's pale glow,
The sacrifice, the agony you may never show.
To give all you have until nothing remains,
To bleed willingly, embracing the pains.

Love is no gentle, weightless flight,

But clawing hands in endless night.

Choosing the battles worth the scars,
And knowing when to surrender to the stars.

Sometimes, love is finding the one
Who can hold your heart when the storm's begun.
Someone worth the torment and the tears,
Who banishes your demons, silences your fears.

But know, no being will erase every ache,
No hand can undo the heartbreaks you make.
Yet you must find the one who, through the fray,
Can lift the sting and guide it away.

Love is not perfection, nor eternal light;
It is the fire that burns through the night.
So seek the one worth the wounds you bear,
The one who lingers when shadows tear.

For in the end, love is not just bliss;
It is the darkened edge, the lingering kiss.
Find the one worth fighting for, who won't fade away,
The one who stays at the end of the day.

Thoughts of a Child

As I lay there on that first cool night,
A spark of love turned into spite.

I prayed in silence, thoughts so still,
Yet shadows crept, bringing a chill.

I wondered if you'd soon return,
Or if your love had ceased to burn.

Were you beneath the same pale moon?
Or had you left my world too soon?

Alone, afraid, I called your name,
Yet silence answered, just the same.

If tears had fallen in the night,
Would anyone have seen my plight?

ACTAEA PACHYPODA

The Edge of Night

I can endure the lash of physical pain,
But my soul is torn, unraveled by the strain.
My eyes, raw rivers, bleed through the night,
Struggling to stay open against the waning light.

I drift in a fog, unsure what to do,
Each choice a dagger, each thought untrue.
What I desire now would undo it all,
Topple the fragile kingdom I've built, let it fall.

I wish the ache would dissolve, take flight,
But it clings like shadows to the edge of night.
This hurt, this darkness, consumes my breath,
A constant companion, a whisper of death.

When I was young, my heart stood tall,
Its storms a veil to mask the fall.

But now I trade scars for a fleeting reprieve,
Physical pain, the solace I choose to deceive.

Alone, I wander, lost in this maze,
Afraid of the silence, trapped in its haze.
No one sees how deeply I bleed,
No one hears my silent plea.

I doubt they could ever truly know,
The depths of anguish, the weight below.
Please take this torment, this endless decay,
Lift me from the abyss—let the shadows fall away.

For I am scared, abandoned, and bare,
Carrying a burden too heavy to bear.
In this cavern of sorrow, I beg and pray,

For the night to retreat and bring the day.

The Final Lament

Their presence remains, but they no longer own me.
The echoes call, but they do not break me.
I have carried sorrow like an unshakable weight,
        But tonight, I let it slip away.

For too long, I was haunted by another's absence,
Defined by a love that never came.
I searched for answers in shadows and silence,
        But some questions are not meant to be tamed.

I have made peace with what cannot be changed.
I have forgiven the ones that let me go.
I have unshackled myself from yesterday's chains.
        And stepped forward into something of my own.

The past still lingers, but I do not bow to it.
The throb still hums, but I do not drown in it.
I have built a life from the ruins they left,
        And in that life, I write.

This is my final lament.
        I will not mourn the loss of me.

The Love That Was Always There

I never thought I would find true love.
I chased fire, mistook passion for something real,
Lost myself in the arms of men
Who only left me burned.

But all along, love was waiting—
Not in stolen kisses, not in empty words,
But in two small hands reaching for mine.

My son, the one who made me a mother,
The moment I held you in my arms, I fell—
Not into ruin, but into love that saved me.
I searched for something I never needed.
You were enough.

My daughter, so wild, so kind,
You taught me what unconditional love really meant.
When you pulled away, I learned—
Real love waits, lets you be,
Loves you from a distance until you're ready to see.

My children taught me to love myself.
If not just for me, then so they would know—
        They are worthy of love that does not break,
                That does not leave,
                        That does not burn.

Nymphaea lotus

SHEILA RUBY

Author Bio

 *Sheila Ruby is a writer based in Ohio, where she lives with her children, and their two dogs. She is the author of A Brief Silence, a memoir, and continues to explore storytelling through poetry and prose.*

SHEILA RUBY

www.ingramcontent.com/pod-product-compliance
Lightning Source LLC
Chambersburg PA
CBHW051337120626
46547CB00016B/2577